Responsible Pet Care

Parrots

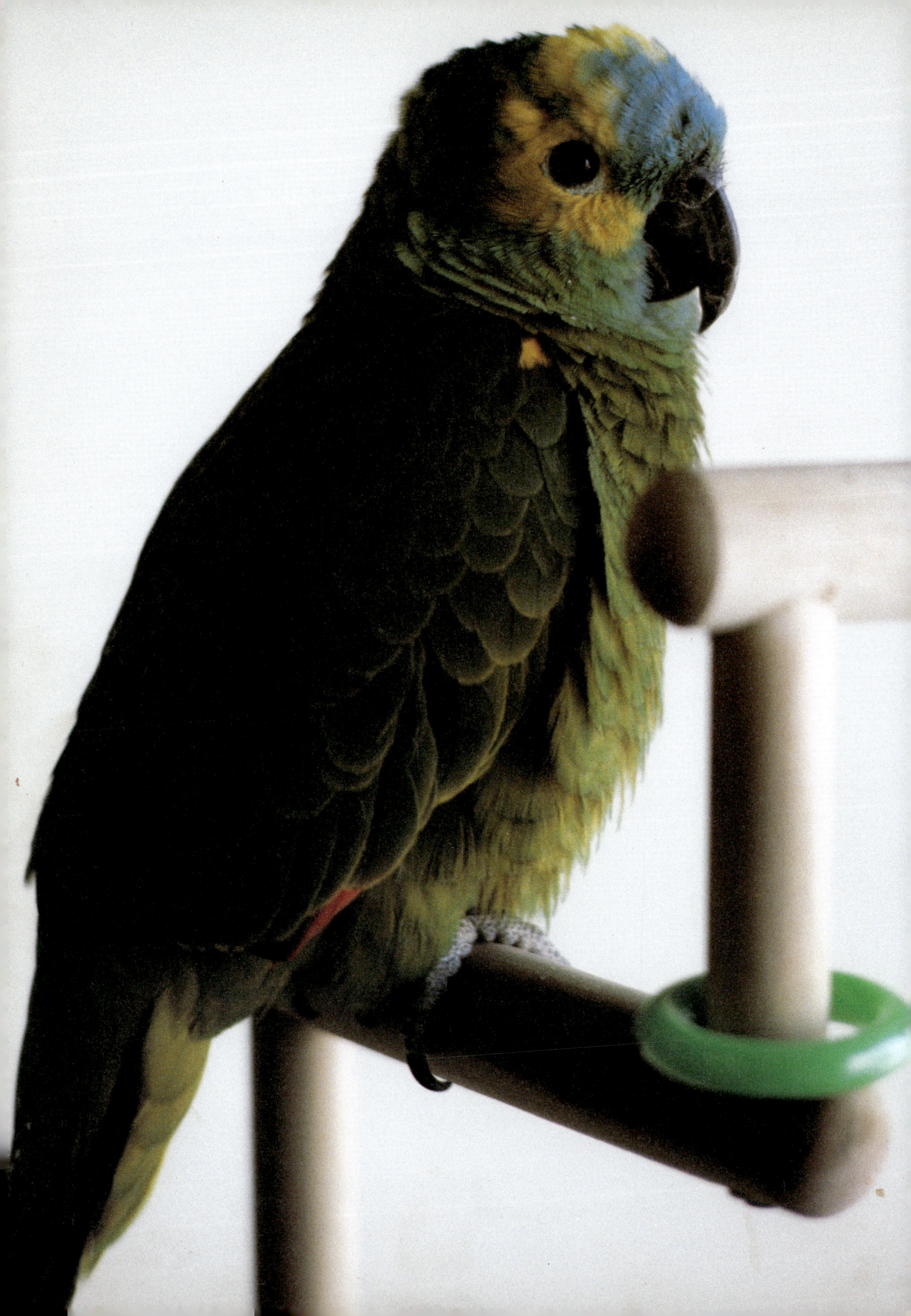

Responsible Pet Care

Parrots

CARLIENNE FRISCH

Rourke Publications, Inc.
Vero Beach, FL 32964

© **1991 Rourke Publications, Inc.**

All rights reserved. No part of this book may be reproduced or utilized in any form or by any means, electronic or mechanical including photocopying, recording or by any information storage and retrieval system without permission in writing from the publisher.

Library of Congress Cataloging-in-Publication Data

Frisch, Carlienne, 1944–
    Parrots / by Carlienne A. Frisch
      p. cm. – (Responsible pet care)
    Includes bibliographical references.
    Summary: Discusses various aspects of caring for a pet parrot, including selection, housing, feeding, grooming, and training.
    ISBN 0-86625-190-1
    1. Parrots–Juvenile literature. [1. Parrots.] I. Title. II. Series: Responsible pet care (Vero Beach, Fla.)
SF473.P3F75 1991
636.6'865–dc20   90-25838
                                                                                  CIP
                                                                                   AC

CONTENTS

1	Is a Parrot For You?	6
2	Varieties of Parrots	8
3	Choosing a Parrot	10
4	The Aviary	12
5	The Cage	14
6	Feeding and Watering	16
7	Care and Handling	18
8	Grooming and Exercise	20
9	Training	22
10	Health and Ailments	24
11	Travel and Exhibiting	26
12	Breeding	27
13	The Young	28
	Glossary	30
	Index	31

Is A Parrot For You?

Parrots are beautiful and intelligent pets. They are best known as "the birds that talk." There are over 300 different kinds of parrots in the world, but only a few **species** are commonly kept as pets.

Parrots are usually kept in either aviaries or cages. Caged parrots forget how to fly, but they soon learn again if freed in an **aviary**.

Parrots require less care than a dog or cat, but they need a lot of human contact or the company of another pet. They have strong likes and dislikes. Parrots often show their displeasure with their claws and beaks. When mistreated, they can be dangerous and can hurt a person badly. Because parrots have long memories, they may even "punish" a person for previous mistreatment. A parrot doesn't have the forgiving nature of many other kinds of pets.

The cockatiel is a small parrot originally from Australia. It has a crested yellow head.

A blue-crown conure "kisses" its owner.

A parrot also can be an affectionate companion. With proper treatment, a pet parrot can form a very strong attachment to a person, another bird, or an animal. A well cared for parrot will climb on your arm and shoulder, nuzzle your head, and mutter to you.

Before getting a parrot, a family must consider several things. Who will feed and clean up after the bird? How will the bird get proper exercise, and who will give the parrot attention and training? Will other pets accept it, and will the parrot's loud "talking" upset neighbors? Who will take care of it when the family is on vacation?

No two parrots are alike; each bird needs an owner who will spend time getting to know the pet. It's best if the owner has had previous experience with a smaller bird, such as a parakeet. You should also know that parrots usually are expensive to purchase and may cost up to $300 a year to feed.

A parrot can be fun to watch, listen to, and train. It can be an interesting companion that talks and does tricks.

Varieties of Parrots

In nature, most parrots live in the forests of hot countries found in Central and South America, Africa, and Australia. Some are able to live in colder areas, such as the mountains of New Zealand. Flocks of wild parrots in Europe come from parrots that were brought to Europe and escaped.

There are eight different kinds of parrots. Most—but not all—come in bright colors, like green, red, blue, yellow, and white.

Small parrots with long tails, such as budgerigars and lovebirds, are called parakeets. African grey parrots, from the Sahara desert, are not bright-colored. They are popular pets because they are good talkers and affectionate when raised in captivity. They live for 30–70 years.

African grey parrots can live up to 70 years.

Macaws can be a lot of work, but they are smart and affectionate pets. Pictured above is a blue and gold macaw.

Many of the 26 species of Amazon parrots are talkative and entertaining once they are five years old. They can be unpredictable and aggressive, however. They live up to 70 years.

Macaws range in size from a dwarf species, such as the Hahn macaw, to the largest of parrots. A macaw is very intelligent and can be playful and affectionate. It also is demanding and very noisy. Macaws must have adequate space for wing exercise. If allowed to fly loose in the house, it will often cause damage to furniture. A macaw lives for up to 70 years. Despite being a challenge to an owner, a macaw will thrive in the hands of an experienced bird handler.

Mynahs **mimic** everyday sounds, such as a ringing phone or a dog barking. They live for up to 25 years. Cockatoos need lots of affection. Hanging parrots, which sleep upside-down, also require substantial attention. Although quite small, they live best in an aviary.

Lories and lorikeets, which are smaller than lories, feed on nectar. Lories are mainly red, while lorikeets are mainly green.

Choosing A Parrot

Domestically raised birds make the best pets. Avoid getting an imported parrot, even one that was caught when young. Many wild-caught birds have fatal diseases which are not detected during the **quarantine** period. They may die several months after completing a quarantine. If you do get an imported bird, however, get a copy of the quarantine certificate.

Even domestically raised birds should be bought only from a reputable breeder. You may wait several months for the species you want, but a chick bred in captivity will make the best life-long companion for you. You also can buy a young bird through ads in magazines such as *Bird Talk* or *American Cage-Bird*. For help in finding breeders, you may contact the American Federation of Aviculture in Phoenix, Arizona.

Cockatoos are showy birds that thrive on attention. This is an umbrella cockatoo.

Parrots enjoy the company of other parrots. At left is a yellow-naped Amazon, and at right, a blue-fronted Amazon.

Before you buy, find out if the bird prefers men or women; many birds have a definite preference. A healthy bird will have eyes that are shiny, smooth feathers, clean nostrils, quiet breathing, and one leg tucked under its body when perched. Wheezing, pumping movements of the tail, or a soft, oddly shaped, or crusty beak all are signs of illness.

Get a written privilege of return in case the bird is not approved by a veterinarian. Many birds, especially the large parrots such as macaws and African greys, should have an **electrocardiogram** (EKG). A veterinarian probably will recommend an EKG for any parrot that has shortness of breath, weakness, or other signs of poor health.

A bird bred in captivity will have a closed band, or ring, on one leg. You can remove the ring with pliers after you decide to keep the bird. Your bill of sale should list the bird's band number, date of your purchase, conditions of sale, price, birth date, and a full description of the parrot's species, sex, and color. It's also important to ask the seller for care and feeding instructions.

The Aviary

An aviary is an enclosure, like a very large cage, usually used for keeping birds outdoors. In cold climates, aviaries need to be built indoors. Parrots are **social birds** that enjoy living in an aviary with other parrots.

Birds kept in an aviary must be checked every morning, and again at dusk before they go to **roost**, for signs of illness. A sick bird must be separated immediately from other birds.

An aviary should have a concrete floor, a strong wood or metal framework, a welded mesh roof and sides, and covered areas that provide shelter and privacy. Perches are needed for roosting. It's a good idea to have a small feeding hatch to reduce the risk of a parrot escaping at feeding time. Build the aviary where it can be seen from the house, but where the parrots will not disturb neighbors. In some communities, you will need a building permit.

You can't have too many perches in an aviary!

This umbrella cockatoo is playing with one of its favorite toys—the lock for its aviary.

Proper construction will keep out rodents. If these pests do get in, place poison or traps only where the birds cannot reach them. Remove all food at night to discourage rodents.

Parrot theft is not unusual. Lock the aviary with a padlock and have strong hardware on the door. A covered pen surrounding the aviary, with a dog in it at night, also helps.

Some parrots can be kept outdoors, even in winter, except in the northern states. Check with a veterinarian or the American Federation of Aviculture before building a year-round aviary.

Parrots that winter outside will need infrared lamps as protection from drafts (which are deadly) and frostbite. Extra-wide perches help prevent frostbite, but you should check each morning for signs of swelling feet or blood on the perches. A bird with frostbite should be brought indoors. To catch a bird in an aviary, use a special bird net.

The Cage

A parrot's cage must have enough space for the bird to stretch its wings completely and to move about freely. The cage should be sturdy. Place it away from drafts, gas fumes, or other odors. It's important to locate it where the parrot can watch people go about their activities. The bird also will need an area of the cage in which to eat, drink, and sleep in privacy.

Commercially made cages can be expensive. It's not hard to make a cage with a melamine or marine plywood base and 12-gauge welded mesh. The mesh openings should be 3 x 1 inches. It is best to make a flat-top cage that is at least 3 x 2 x 2 feet. The size of the cage will depend on the size of the bird. For example, a macaw needs a cage nearly 4 x 3 x 2 feet.

A parrot's cage should be placed out of the way, but where the bird can observe people's activities. If you put the cage near a window, make sure there's no draft.

Natural branches make the best perches.

A mesh floor will allow droppings and spilled food to fall onto newspapers or cat litter placed below the mesh. You can also place a tray in the bottom of the cage, but it must be cleaned daily. The entire cage should be scrubbed thoroughly once a week.

The cage should be placed about four feet from the floor on a solid base. During warm weather, it can be hung outdoors. Make sure the bird cannot reach plants that are poisonous or that have been sprayed with chemicals. An outdoor cage needs protection from wind, rain, and sun. To provide this, cover part of the sides and roof with opaque material, such as marine plywood.

Horizontal bars in the cage give the bird an opportunity to climb and exercise. Natural branches are better than plastic for this, but they should be replaced as soon as the bark is chewed off. Wooden spools and blocks, small cowbells, rawhide bones, and artificial dog bones make good toys. Be sure not to give the parrot an object on which it may choke.

Before designing the cage and choosing toys, it is a good idea to look at several kinds of cages and toys at a pet supply store.

Feeding And Watering

Parrots are mainly seed-eating birds. About 60 percent of their diet can be sunflower seeds. In addition to sunflower seeds, offer canary and hemp seed, unhulled rice, and cracked corn. Parrots also enjoy washed fruit and vegetables, corn on the cob, a cooked bone, and whole-grain bread with peanut butter. Cuttlebone or toasted eggshells provide minerals in the diet.

Most parrots can also be fed pellet bird food. Transition from a seed and fruit diet will take several days, however. Many birds find a pellet diet boring, and even those that accept it will need the variety of additional fruit, vegetables, and small amounts of hard cheese, meat, fish, or hard-boiled eggs.

A parrot's diet should consist mainly of seeds, but it also likes fruits and vegetables. This is a yellow-naped Amazon.

Food and water containers should be fastened securely to the side of the cage.

Parrots need grit in their diet. Birds use grit to grind food in the gizzard, or stomach. Commercial bird grit, which is available in pet stores, consists of quartz and other natural ingredients. A grit known as mineral grit can provide additional minerals for the parrot's diet.

A parrot needs a constant supply of clean, fresh drinking water. Some bird owners use bottled water or boiled tap water. This eliminates chemicals that are added to the water supply in many communities.

Fasten food and water containers to the bars of the cage so they cannot be tipped. In an aviary, hook the containers onto the mesh near the feeding hatch, or build a revolving shelf of food containers so you can add food and water from outside.

Care And Handling

When a parrot arrives in a new home, it needs time to rest. It's also important to have fresh food and water ready. The owner must be patient and gentle. Parrots appreciate a daily routine in their feeding, watering, and cage cleaning. These should be done at the same time every day to prevent stressing the parrot. Young children must be taught how to treat a parrot properly. An unhappy parrot can be dangerous or self-destructive. Biting, feather plucking, toe chewing, and various medical problems all can result from stress.

Parrots may bite if they're afraid, mad, or excited. A parrot that bites for no reason will usually not change its ways. Other biters can be cured of their habit. Some parrots go through a stage at six months when they bite from excitement. To stop this action, tap the parrot lightly on the beak and sternly say "no." Never hit a parrot; this will make the problem worse.

Some parrots bite out of excitement.

To stop a parrot from biting, tap its beak lightly and sternly say, "no."

To catch a parrot that gets loose, use a net. After catching the bird, place your thumb and forefinger on either side of the beak to hold it closed. Wrap the bird in a towel while holding its beak shut. Then gently remove it from the net.

Talk to your pet and let it out of its cage often. Once you are friends, put your hand slowly and fearlessly into the cage. The parrot will step onto your finger. A creature of habit, the bird will expect you to use the same hand, in the same position, every time. A parrot will leave the cage on its own and will return when ready, but it will enjoy your attention in doing so.

A parrot that cannot take a full bath to keep its feathers in good condition should be sprayed with warm water from a plant mister. After a few times, the bird will look forward to this by ruffling its feathers excitedly. A parrot also dips its head in water to indicate it wants a bath.

Grooming and Exercise

Parrots preen, or groom, themselves. They use their beaks to clean and smooth their feathers. They spend many hours reattaching separated barbs on their feathers and putting the feathers back into position. A parrot spreads oil on its feathers from a gland near the base of its tail. This keeps the feathers healthy and makes them waterproof.

Parrots **molt**, or lose their feathers, once a year at about the same time each year. Each bird has its own molting schedule. Stress can bring on a partial or early molt. Normally, a molt is gradual, with new feathers coming in as old feathers continue dropping off. A stressed bird, however, may pluck out its feathers. This is a sign of a problem and is not part of a normal molt.

This blue and gold macaw has started to molt on its breast. Parrots molt once a year; each bird has its own schedule.

A parrot exercises its beak and toes on the perch of its cage.

Birds in an aviary can get enough exercise, but a caged parrot needs free-flight time in its routine. You must, however, keep it out of trouble. To prevent accidents, close all doors, windows, and toilets. Cover any open fireplace. Cover mirrors and close drapes on any windows without net curtains so the bird doesn't fly into the glass and break its neck. Keep the parrot out of the kitchen. Remove cacti, poisonous plants, matches (which are toxic), felt-tipped markers, pens, and pencils.

Make sure the parrot does not bite into an electrical cord. Do not use aerosols or an electric fan in any room in which the parrot can fly. Keep an eye on the parrot when there are other pets around. Leave the cage door open so the parrot can return on its own. You may offer it a treat of favorite food to coax it into the cage.

A parrot will exercise its beak and toes on the perches in its cage. It will enjoy clean, dry perches of various sizes. Never chain a bird to a perch.

Training

After a few days with you, your parrot will be ready to begin trusting you. Spend the first week trying to get the bird to perch on your gloved hand or a stick, such as a broom handle. In 15-minute sessions (two or three times a day), put your hand or stick gently upward where the parrot's chest and legs join. The parrot will grasp on with its beak and then with its legs. If you use a stick, ease your hand under the stick, feeding the parrot tidbits with your free hand. When the bird is on your finger, slowly take it from the cage. At first, the parrot will jump back to its perch, but after enough practice, it will stay on your finger. It will then be **finger-tame**.

If the parrot tries to nip your hand, push its chin away with your other hand, saying "no" sternly. If the bird flies off your finger, wait until it perches and then offer it your finger again.

This blue-crown conure is finger-tame.

African grey parrots aren't as colorful as other parrots, but they are good talkers and affectionate pets.

Parrots can be taught to "talk" or mimic voices and sounds. A young, tame, contented bird will be the best talker. Some parrots, such as small macaws, begin mimicking at a young age. Others may be nine months old. Most parrots learn five or six words, others many more. Males learn more words, and faster, than females. Parrots can learn from listening to other parrots, from a human teacher, or from a tape player.

To start, choose a short, simple phrase, such as "hello" or "get ready." Repeat it three or four times whenever you pass the parrot's cage. In addition, have two or three 10-minute sessions daily, repeating the phrase with no distractions, such as a TV in the background.

Most parrots speak in one voice, but some mimic people's voices or household sounds. Some birds associate a word with an action or sound. For example, they will say "hello" when someone arrives or the phone rings, even though they don't understand the meaning of their words.

Health and Ailments

An unhappy parrot acts agitated, squawks constantly, or repeats motions, such as rocking or bowing. A sick parrot, on the other hand, is listless. It may sit with closed eyes and ruffled feathers. Droppings might be watery. The bird might refuse to eat or may scratch excessively.

A sick parrot needs extra warmth, peace and quiet, and its favorite food. Seek advice from a veterinarian. The vet may prescribe antibiotics, or recommend force-feeding. The vet might also suggest using an infrared lamp to provide additional heat.

Parrots can get several diseases. Newcastle disease can be prevented by vaccination. Psittacosis (parrot fever) responds to antibiotics. Psittacine beak and feather disease is treated by controlling infections and providing vitamin and mineral supplements. Pacheco's disease, caused by a herpes virus, requires antibiotics, vitamin C, and lots of loving care. Parrots can also get avian pox, which may cause sudden death. A veterinarian can teach you the warning signs of these diseases.

The white object inside this cage is a cuttlebone, which is actually the internal shell of a cuttlefish. A cuttlebone provides a parrot with essential minerals.

Pay close attention to changes in your parrot's mood. A listless bird is probably sick, and needs prompt care from a veterinarian. This macaw is very healthy!

Parasites such as roundworms may infect a parrot. A veterinarian can test **stool samples** for these worms. Cleanliness helps prevent them. An infected parrot may not suffer, but it can lose weight and have runny droppings. More seriously, it may develop an intestinal blockage.

Red mites, which are gray until they turn red after eating blood, live on surfaces around parrots. They may live on parrot chicks, causing their deaths. Red mites can be controlled with the use of special chemicals.

Blindness, caused by injury, infection, poisoning, or old age, usually will not affect a parrot's quality of life. Most will continue to enjoy food and attention.

Like other health problems, abscesses, tumors, fractured legs and wings, or poisoning all require a veterinarian's attention. Less seriously, some birds may need their toenails or beaks trimmed. A veterinarian can do this or can advise the owner on how to do it.

Travel and Exhibiting

Parrots travel well in a car. Keep the bird in its cage and take along a cage cover, food, and the bird's toys. Bring water from home or use bottled water. Check in advance if the hotels and motels in which you plan to stay will allow your parrot in the room. Never leave the bird in a car during hot or cold weather.

If you are traveling by airplane, try to arrange to have your bird in its cage with you. Shipping a bird in a non-passenger section is not recommended.

You should find out if the communities you plan to visit require a veterinarian's health certificate for your parrot. Foreign countries may have a six-month quarantine.

If you exhibit your parrot in a bird show, you probably will be able to leave it in its own cage if the cage meets show standards. The cage must be a certain size and usually must be painted white inside and black outside. Find out requirements in advance. Parrots are judged on appearance in some shows, and on their talking ability in other shows. You will want to decide how to show off your parrot to its best advantage.

An umbrella cockatoo extends its head feathers.

Breeding

For some parrot owners, breeding is the most important and rewarding part of owning a parrot. It provides domestically raised birds for other parrot owners. The young birds can be advertised in the magazines mentioned in the third chapter.

To make sure you have a male and female, have a veterinarian examine the birds. Be aware that some of the large species, such as Amazons, African greys, macaws, and cockatoos, are not easily bred. For advice on breeding parrots, contact the Association of Avian Veterinarians, P.O. Box 299, East Northport, New York 11731.

Parrots lay two to nine white eggs in a **clutch**, depending on the species. The parents will take turns sitting on the nest for 24 to 30 days. You must make sure they have water baths available during this time. If any eggs disappear, one of the parents is an egg-eater. Watch to determine which bird is guilty and remove it from the nest immediately. If the **incubation** goes well, you will have parrot chicks within a month.

Parrots will not mate unless they feel secure and are paired with a compatible partner. Pictured here is a mated pair of cockatiels.

The Young

Parrot chicks are completely helpless when hatched. Their eyes and ears are closed. They are naked except for **down**, which varies from a few wisps to a heavy covering, depending on the species. The chicks must stay in the nest with their parents to keep warm.

The owner should add wood shavings daily to the bottom of the nesting box to help keep it clean. If the parents are used to the nest being handled, they will not desert their young.

Parrot chicks are fed by their parents until they learn to fly. If the parents don't feed a chick, it may mean the chick is weak or sick and will not grow into a healthy bird. The parents know this by instinct.

Sometimes first-time parents don't know that they should feed their chicks. If this happens, you can hand-raise the chicks. Although it is time-consuming, it results in very tame young birds for which there is great demand as pets.

These cockatiels are six weeks old. Their box is attached to their parents' cage.

Could this playful macaw be winking at the photographer?

Remove the chicks from the nest if you notice that the parents aren't feeding them. In a cool climate, put them in a **brooder**. A box with a heating pad is adequate in a warm climate.

Use a spoon with the sides bent inward to feed the chicks. Never fill the birds' **crops** full. Feed chicks between 6:30 a.m. and 11 p.m. to stay with their natural sleep cycle. Newly hatched chicks need food every 90 minutes. Older chicks need thicker food every three to four hours.

For the food, make a mixture of dry baby cereal (at least 15 percent protein) and fruit or canned baby food. Blend well with water, then heat thoroughly. Add mineral supplements, such as calcium, to keep heat from destroying their nutritional value. At 10 days, add wheat germ and sunflower seed kernels. Wean the chicks gradually from soft food to seeds.

The chicks' eyes open at about three weeks, their ears a few days later. Some parrots get a second layer of down at about four weeks; most have their full **plumage** by the time they are two months old.

GLOSSARY

Aviary	A large, enclosed area for keeping birds. An aviary is usually located outdoors.
Brooder	A heated box for raising young birds.
Clutch	The eggs laid in one breeding period; also the group of baby birds hatched from those eggs.
Crop	A pouch-like part of a bird's throat in which food is held and softened.
Down	Soft, fine feathers.
Electrocardiogram (EKG)	A laboratory test of the heart.
Finger-tame	Tame enough to perch on a finger.
Incubation	The time during which eggs are kept warm so they will hatch.
Mimic	To imitate speech or action.
Molt	To drop old feathers at certain times of the year and replace them with new ones.
Plumage	The feathers of a bird.
Quarantine	A strict isolation intended to prevent the spread of disease.
Roost	To settle or stay for the night; a perch upon which birds rest at night.
Social birds	Birds that enjoy the company of other birds, animals, or people.
Species	A group of related animals or plants.
Stool sample	A sample of the feces or droppings.

INDEX

African grey parrot	8	Illness	12, 13, 24
Amazon parrots	9		
American Cage-bird	10	Life span	8, 9
American Federation		Lories	9
of Aviculture	10, 13	Lorikeets	9
Aviary	6, 9, 12		
		Macaws	9
Bath	19	Molting	20
Beaks	25	Mynahs	9
Behavior	6, 7, 18, 19		
Bird Talk	10	Nest	27, 28
Breeding	27		
		Parakeets	8
Cage	6, 14, 15, 19	Parasites	25
Chicks	28, 29	Perches	12, 13, 21
Cleaning	15, 18	Preening	20
Cockatoos	9		
Colors	8	Showing	26
Cost	7	Species	6, 9
Cuttlebone	16	Stress	18, 20
Diet	16	Talking	7, 8, 23
Drafts	13, 14	Toenails	25
		Toys	15
Eggs	27	Training	22, 23
Exercise	21	Travel	26
Feathers	20	Varieties of parrots	8
Food	16, 29	Veterinarian	11, 13, 24, 25
Grit	17	Water	17
Grooming	20		
Handling	18, 19		
Health	11, 24		

Photographs by Susan Eckhoff: 6, 15, 27, 28
All other photographs by Mark E. Ahlstrom

*We would like to thank the following people
and businesses for their help in making this book:*

Randy Beinke
Peter Eckhoff
The Fish Bowl
Mark Hanson
Gayle Harrtranft
Tom and Donna Moore
Kathy Weinstein

Produced by Mark E. Ahlstrom
(The Bookworks)
St. Peter, MN

Typesetting and Keylining: The Final Word
Photo Research: Judith A. Ahlstrom